Praise for *Driven for Success:*

"If you are pursuing the abundant opportunity that Young Living offers, you absolutely must understand the compensation plan in order to take advantage of all the income possibilities. Thanks to the man behind Oily Tools, Jake has created this MUST-READ tool to help you fully understand the compensation plan in an easy and interactive way. I highly recommend this book!"

Alana Bookhout

"Driven For Success: Road Map To The Comp Plan" is an essential guide that every distributor should have. Whether you are building a business now or thinking of sharing this opportunity with others and making a little money on the side, this guide will give you a clear understanding of the many ways that Young Living will reward you for sharing Wellness, Purpose and Abundance. Jake clarifies the topics of commissions (which reward you for sharing), and the many bonuses, which provide incentives for building your Young Living business the right way."

Daniel Erickson

"This book is by far one of the most comprehensive yet engaging texts on the Young Living compensation plan that I've ever read. It is crucial for all Young Living members, new and seasoned, to have a copy of this book, and to reference it often for the betterment of their businesses."

DRIVEN
FOR SUCCESS

ROAD MAP TO THE COMP PLAN

JAKE DEMPSEY

This book may be purchased in bulk for educational, business, fund-raising, or sales promotional use. For book orders visit imdrivenforsuccess.com.

© 2015 Licensed2Live, LLC
Published by Licensed2Live, LLC
Southlake, Texas

ISBN 978-1-4951-6889-5

Cover & Layout designed by Michael Durham at designerMD.net.

Printed In the United States of America.

To purchase copies of this book please visit imdrivenforsuccess.com.

Contents

Acknowledgment

Dear Kristy (my loving wife),

Thank you for being such a kind and wonderful person, and not admitting that you are way out of my league! To everyone else, direct all complaints to Kristy as this book was her idea.

Introduction

This is not a secret manual or treasure map, but rather a simple and straightforward road map that explains how you can earn income with Young Living. In this manual, we will cover key concepts, including terminology that you will read throughout this book. Each major compensation structure is discussed in simple terms, with examples and pictures that will help solidify your understanding. You will also find tips along the way that we hope will help you think more deeply about the content. This is not just a reading experience! You will also find exercises to practice what you've learned. All you will need is a calculator, scratch paper, and *Driven for Success*!

I'll make an educated guess and say that you are already using Young Living products and have discovered the wellness they bring. You might even be recommending these wonderful products to your friends and family, and are now curious about how you might financially benefit when inviting others into this wonderful opportunity.

But, what is this wonderful opportunity? How do you actually earn money? How much can you earn? The great news is that through this material we will journey into these questions and many more together. Why am I excited? I am excited because you have made a decision to apply energy into finding out!

"The secret of change is to focus all of your energy, not on fighting the old, but on building the new."

- Socrates

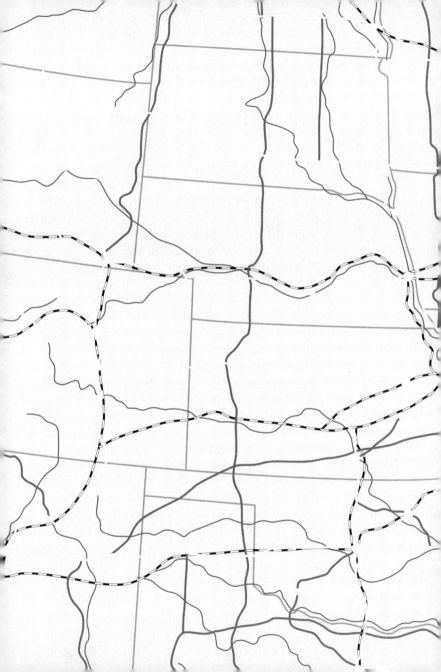

WEBSTER WOULD BE PROUD

Let's start by covering some key ideas and vocabulary that you will see throughout this book. Instead of just providing you with definitions, we will go over each key word and dive a bit deeper into its meaning and purpose.

Retail Customer

A Retail Customer is considered a person who has joined Young Living with the intention of purchasing products at retail price for personal use and has no current desire to begin sharing as an income opportunity. They are ready for wellness but may not yet be ready to explore the income potential our company provides. Because you are reading this book, I am sure you are thinking, "Why buy at retail? Why don't they leverage this income opportunity?" Those are great questions! A person new to Young Living may solely be seeking wellness or may not even know a business opportunity exists. This is ok! What excites me about these people is that over time, as they use the products, they naturally begin to recommend the products to their friends and family. This is when they are more likely to listen to the idea of pursuing Young Living as a business. Young Living allows existing Retail Customers to convert to Wholesale Members at any time! I like to think of Retail Customers as future Wholesale Members and you should too!

❝ I like to think of Retail Customers as future Wholesale Members and you should too! ❞

Wholesale Member

It is my hope that you are included in this category. A Wholesale Member is a person who has decided they would like to purchase products at 24% off the retail price. You are also eligible to take advantage of Essential Rewards, which we will go over later. These two elements alone are usually enough to persuade someone to sign up as a Wholesale Member. In addition to these two benefits, Wholesale Members are also eligible to participate in the Young Living income opportunity. Initially, your new signups may not be interested in the business. Believe it

> **"Wholesale Members are eligible to participate in the Young Living income opportunity."**

or not, this is not uncommon. When speaking to business builders, I have heard more times than not that they did not intend on growing a Young Living business. Our personal story is that Kristy and I also did not intend on growing a Young Living business. When we were ready to take advantage of the opportunity, it was right there waiting on us as Wholesale Members!

Enroller

A key activity in any network marketing business is inviting others to take a look at your products and/or your business opportunity. When you recruit a new team member you are listed

> **"A key activity in any network marketing business is inviting others..."**

as their enroller. You are the person responsible for introducing the new person to Young Living. Later in this book we will cover specific compensation structures that are provided to the enroller for introducing new members to Young Living. It is possible to be the enroller of a new member and not the sponsor. This occurs when a member has been strategically placed in your downline by someone in your upline or the new member has made a request to Young Living for you to be their sponsor. Young Living has rules around sponsor changes that can be found in the Policies and Procedures (P&P) document. You can request this from Young Living or ask your upline where the current version of P&P can be found.

Sponsor

When growing your network marketing business you need support; you also want to provide support to others. Your sponsor is your direct upline and the person that should provide you with the daily support you require. In a network marketing business, it is possible that your sponsor is no longer pursuing the business. In this case, you can get support from their sponsor. Because of this, you may also be providing support to a member in your organization that you are not directly sponsoring. It is possible to be a member's sponsor, but not their enroller. This occurs when a member has been strategically placed in your downline by someone in your upline, or the new member has made a request to Young Living for you to be their sponsor. Young Living has rules around sponsor changes that can be found in the Policies and Procedures document. You can request this from Young Living or ask your upline where the current version of P&P can be found.

PV

You are now in a global sales organization! PV (Personal Volume) is a number used to communicate the commissionable value of any product in the Young Living catalog and is not affected by the currency of a specific market. Young Living has members (Retail Customers and Wholesale Members) all over the globe, and in order to create a unified value for calculating commissions and rank, every product is assigned a PV amount. A product will have a price that varies by market but its PV value remains constant. The PV amount does not always equal the sales price, and in some cases no PV value is assigned to a product.

> **" A product will have a price that varies by market but its PV value remains constant. "**

Generally speaking, when commissions are calculated, the PV is the value used, not the retail prices of the products sold. Customer Commissions are the only commissions paid where the retail price of the product matters. We will discuss Customer Commissions in a later section.

PGV

The PGV (Personal Group Volume) refers to the sales volume of all members up to the first Silver+ leader in each leg. It also includes your own personal PV. If you have legs that are qualifying you for a specific rank, those legs are not used in the calculation of PGV. When building your team, you have to ensure you have enough non-qualifying legs to help you meet the PGV requirement for each rank since the qualifying legs do not count towards the PGV calculation.

OGV

Now that you are building your network marketing empire, you will begin to sponsor other Wholesale Members and Retail Customers. Your OGV (Organizational Group Volume) is the total PV of all the members (customer and wholesale) that exist in your organization. OGV, like PV and PGV, are used as qualifications for rank in Young Living.

EXERCISE YOUR BRAIN!

Use your new knowledge to calculate the PV, PGV, and OGV for the person at the top of this downline. In the graphic we have outlined two legs to act as the qualifying legs for this Silver leader.

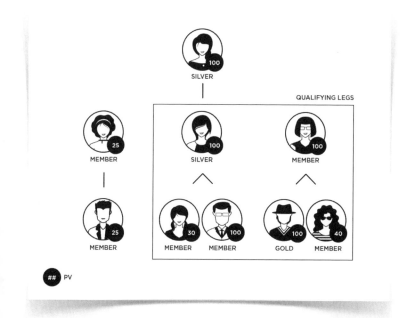

If you answered 100 PV, 150 PGV, and 620 OGV you are well on your way to being a compensation super star!

Chapter 2

RANKS

Now that you have a clear understanding of core terms, let's tackle ranks in Young Living. Every month, your rank resets back to zero. Each month, you earn your rank. The qualification categories are the same: PV, OGV, Leg x OGV, and PGV. The difference is in how much in each category is required to reach the desired rank. Below is a table that outlines the qualifications for each rank.

	PV	OGV	LEG x OGV	PGV
Distributor	50			
Star	100	500		
Senior Star	100	2,000		
Executive	100	4,000	2 x 1,000	
Silver	100	10,000	2 x 4,000	1,000
Gold	100	35,000	3 x 6,000	1,000
Platinum	100	100,000	4 x 8,000	1,000
Diamond	100	250,000	5 x 15,000	1,000
Crown Diamond	100	750,000	6 x 20,000	1,000
Royal Crown Diamond	100	1,500,000	6 x 35,000	1,000

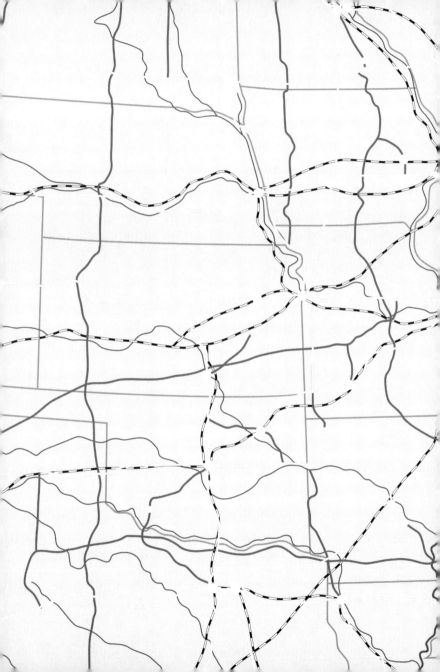

COMPRESSION

A unique component of the Young Living Compensation Plan is Dynamic Compression. Compression occurs when a member in your downline fails to place a 100PV order for the month. Their members, up to and including the first qualifying member, virtually roll up to be on the same level as the member who did not place the 100PV order.

The digram below shows compression in action.

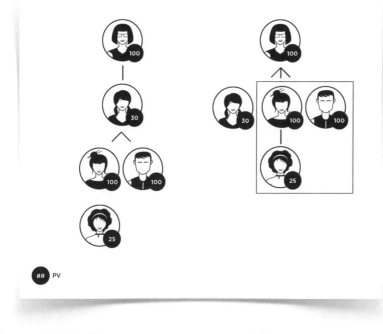

Dynamic Compression occurs for the entire downline. Why is it awesome? Let's pretend that Betty, your personally sponsored member, places a 30PV order and her personally sponsored member Jill places a 100PV order. Since Betty did not place a 100PV order, Jill will compress to your level 1. You now virtually have more level 1 members. This maximizes your Unilevel Commissions and also maximizes your ability to achieve rank, as the new virtual level 1 members can be used as qualifying legs for rank.

An important point to remember is that compression is a virtual process. You can't see this virtual rollup anywhere in your downline. Also, compression isn't permanent, as it is done each month for commission and rank calculations.

Chapter 3

EXERCISE YOUR BRAIN!

Now that you understand compression, take out a scratch piece of paper and redraw this downline as it would look after compression has occurred. Keep in mind that compression occurs to the entire tree.

Later we will talk through Unilevel Commissions and you will see how this unique component of the compensation plan is a powerful mechanism to maximize your earnings.

Chapter 4

QUALIFICATIONS

There are numerous avenues for generating income in Young Living. The compensation plan consists of multiple structures: Customer Commissions, Unilevel Commissions, Fast Start Bonus, Start Living Bonus, Rising Star Team Bonus, Generation Leadership Bonus, Generation Leadership Commission, and

> **❝ There are numerous avenues for generating income in Young Living. ❞**

Diamond Express. For each of these commission structures there are minimum qualifications that are primarily based on your PV.

50PV
By having at least 50PV for a given month, you are eligible to earn commissions and bonuses in Young Living. At 50PV you are eligible to earn Customer Commissions and enroller-based bonuses, which are the Fast Start Bonus and Start Living Bonus.

100PV
At 100PV you unlock the ability to earn Unilevel Commissions, Rising Star Team Bonus, Generation Leadership Bonus, and Generation Leadership Commission.

100PV + ER (Essential Rewards)
The only commission structure that requires you to be on Essential Rewards is the Rising Star Team Bonus. We will go over this commission structure in great detail, as I feel it is an incredible tool for you to use to not only create a solid foundation for your Young Living business, but it also acts as a powerful duplication tool as well.

Rank

In addition to PV, a few of the commission structures require that you are at a specific rank or higher. For example, in order to earn the Generation Leadership Bonus or Generation Leadership Commission, you must be a rank of Silver or higher. To earn the Diamond Express bonus you must be a rank of Diamond or higher.

Business Building Tip

You love Young Living products, right? You are probably ordering every month but may not have taken the plunge to enroll in Essential Rewards. You may not even know what Essential Rewards is! Simply put, Essential Rewards or ER is a type of autoshipment program. ER allows you to change your order at any point (until it ships) each month, and amazing benefits, like reduced shipping and redeemable points on future product purchases, are part of the plan. As you continue to use ER, you earn a higher percentage of points from your purchases. Nothing is as sweet as placing a big order and spending only ER points! To learn more about ER, contact your sponsor.

> **❝ Nothing is as sweet as placing a big order and spending only ER points! ❞**

Why talk about ER in qualifications? In order to maximize your earning potential, you have to have 100PV and be enrolled in ER to qualify for the Rising Star Team Bonus. Why not just make it easy and commit to placing 100PV on ER each month? This will ensure you are automatically qualified to earn as much as possible!

Now what?

At this point you should have an understanding of the core terminology we will be using throughout the rest of the book. In fact, I want you to stop reading when you have completed this chapter. I know, most authors are probably not going to ask that you put down the book,

but I think this is important. What I'd like for you to do is to take some time and review what you have just read. You may need to read it twice. Review the diagrams and exercises. Make sure you have a solid grasp of the foundational items that you have already read.

We each learn in different ways, and so far we have engaged your learning center by visually reinforcing the content with diagrams, and asking you to critically think by completing each portion's exercises. If you skipped the exercises out of excitement to continue, this is your chance to slow down! In the following chapters, we will dive deeply into each commission structure, and a solid understanding of the prior pages is needed to internalize what comes next!

CUSTOMER COMMISSIONS

If you recall, Retail Customers in Young Living have decided to purchase products at retail price for personal use. Remember, we are going to refer to them as future Wholesale Members!

When you place a qualifying order of 50PV, Young Living pays you the difference between retail and wholesale price. In most cases, this equates to a 24% commission on the retail value of the products

> **" Young Living pays you the difference between retail and wholesale price. "**

purchased. In rare instances, the difference between the retail and wholesale price is not 24%. For example, let's assume Sally purchases a product at retail for $48.00 and that product has a wholesale price of $36.48. If you qualify to earn this commission, you would earn $11.52 in commissions because that is the difference between the retail price and wholesale price or $48.00 - $36.48 = $11.52.

When looking at your virtual office, you won't see the differential information. You will see the PV amount for each customer based on the products they purchased.

For customers that are deeper than your level 1, you also earn a commission. As you rank up, you can earn deeper. The percentages are the same for every level, but you earn more as you rank because you earn deeper. The commission percentages starting at level 2 are 8%, 5%, 4%, 4%. The depth you can earn follows the same pattern as the Unilevel Commission Structure.

Nitty-Gritty

Compression affects Customer Commissions. However, when compression occurs, the maximum amount you can earn on a Retail Customer that you do not sponsor is 8%. For example, if you have a level 2 customer that should compress to your level 1, you can not earn 24% on that customer. Instead, you will be paid the maximum percentage of 8% for your non-sponsored customers.

Chapter 5
EXERCISE YOUR BRAIN!

Now that you know how to calculate Customer Commissions, work the problems below to determine the correct commission amount. Yes, these are word problems, and yes, you can use a calculator and scratch paper!

Example 1

As a Retail Customer, Jennifer loves her Young Living products. Richard, Jennifer's sponsor, gives her a call to see how she is enjoying the Lavender she purchased last month. To Richard's surprise, Jennifer used the last bit of Lavender last night and actually needs to purchase more! The next morning Jennifer purchased three bottles of Lavender, which retail for $30.92 each and have a wholesale price of $23.50. If Richard places a 50PV order, how much Customer Commission will he earn on Jennifer's purchase?

Example 2

Kristy was recently informed that a new Retail Customer enrolled with her personally-sponsored Wholesale Member Amy. The new customer purchased $200.00 in product, which had a wholesale price of $152.00 and a PV of 152. How much in Customer Commissions will Amy earn on this new customer? How much will Kristy earn in Customer Commissions on this new customer?

Answer Key:

Example 1

Richard will earn $22.26 in total Customer Commissions for Jennifer's purchase. We first determine the difference from retail to wholesale on one bottle of oil, which is $30.92 - $23.50 = $7.42. Now that we know how much Richard earns on one bottle, we multiple that by three since Jennifer purchased three bottles.

Example 2

In this example we need to calculate commissions for two people, Kristy and Amy. Let's start with Amy. Since the total order was $200.00 in retail, with a wholesale price of $152.00, we find the difference in the two which would be $200.00 - $152.00. This would give us a total for Amy of $48.00. Amy will earn $48.00 on her new customer in Customer Commissions. Next, we can calculate Kristy's Customer Commissions. Since the new customer is her level 2 member, she will earn 8% on the PV of the customer's purchases. We would take the 152PV x 8% to get a total of $12.16 that Kristy will earn on the new customer in Customer Commissions.

START LIVING BONUS

If you haven't had the chance to share Young Living with a prospect yet, you should do so soon! Not only is it a rewarding experience to share your journey to Wellness, Purpose, and Abundance; it's also fun to share the Young Living story and help new members begin their own personal journeys.

As you share Young Living, you will begin enrolling new members. The Start Living Bonus is Young Living's way of saying thank you for introducing a new person to their products. This bonus is a one-time, $25 bonus paid to the enroller of a new member as long as the new member purchases a Premium Starter Kit in the same calendar month that their account was setup.

> **❝ The Start Living Bonus is Young Living's way of saying thank you for introducing a new person to their products. ❞**

Additionally, if a person converts from a Retail Customer to a Wholesale Member and purchases a Premium Starter Kit, you will be eligible for this bonus. You must have 50PV to qualify for this bonus.

Business Building Tip

Have you heard, "You and me plus three equals free?" It is a great concept! If you enroll a new member, you can help them understand that by hosting their own sharing session and enrolling three new members with a Premium Starter Kit, they can earn in bonuses (Start Living and Fast Start) enough to pay for their own kit.

Are you ready to apply this newfound knowledge? I bet you know what's next!

EXERCISE YOUR BRAIN!

It's time for some old-fashioned word problems! Break out your scratch paper and calculator and work through each of these examples.

Example 1

Sally, having found wellness in her family, decides to share Young Living products with a small group in her home. At the close of the class she enrolls three new members, and all three decide to start their journey with the Premium Starter Kit. In her glee, Sally places her monthly order at 127PV. How much in Start Living Bonus does Sally qualify for?

Example 2

In the line at the DMV, Jennifer applies her favorite oil, Stress Away. She signed up with Young Living a few months ago and on occasion places an order. This month she will not make a purchase. While in line, Brad notices the wonderful aroma and begins to talk with Jennifer about her oils. Time passes and both Jennifer and Brad ease through the DMV without a worry. After the DMV encounter, Brad decides to sign up! Jennifer uses her OilyTools mobile app to send Brad a personal signup link (which includes her member number) to ensure that Brad is enrolled under her. Brad eagerly enrolls and purchases a Premium Starter Kit. How much in Start Living Bonus does Jennifer qualify for?

Example 3

It is New Year's Day and David's phone rings. David just modified his January 3rd ER order to include 400PV of his favorite products. On the other line is his cousin Barbara who learned about essential oils from David's webinar a few days ago. In her excitement, she signed up online as soon as she watched the webinar, but did not complete her sign up. David helps her to purchase her Premium

Starter Kit and she can't wait to get her new oils! How much Start Living Bonus will David qualify for after his ER order processes?

Example 4

Meagan is hosting a small essential oil sharing session after receiving this month's order of 265PV worth of product and is asked by Julie if she can join in on the fun. Julie, a long time Young Living Retail Customer, wants to learn more about Meagan's new products. Meagan enrolls one new member with a Premium Starter Kit, and after learning more about the Wholesale Member discount, Julie decides to convert to a Wholesale Member. Julie converts and purchases a Premium Starter Kit. How much Start Living Bonus does Meagan qualify for?

Answer Key:

Example 1

Sally will qualify for $75 in Start Living Bonus because she has enrolled three new members and all members enrolled with a Premium Starter Kit. Sally has also exceeded the 50PV required for her to qualify for the bonus.

Example 2

Jennifer unfortunately qualifies for $0 in Start Living Bonus. Even though Brad enrolled with a Premium Starter Kit, Jennifer does not qualify to earn the bonus because she has not met the 50PV requirement on her own purchases.

Example 3

David qualifies for $0 in Start Living Bonus. He does exceed the 50PV requirement on his own purchases and even enrolls a new member with a Premium Starter Kit. However, he does not qualify because Barbara did not purchase the Premium Starter Kit in the same month as her sign up.

Example 4

Meagan qualifies for $50 in Start Living Bonus. She exceeded the 50PV requirement on her own purchases. She also enrolled a new member with a Premium Starter Kit, which earns her $25. She earns the additional $25 because she converted Julie, a Retail Customer, to a Wholesale Member who purchased a Premium Starter Kit as well.

Your fifth grade math teacher is smiling from ear-to-ear right now. If you did not get the same answers, take a moment and go back to the examples and dissect them piece-by-piece based on the definition of the Start Living Bonus Commission Structure.

FAST START BONUS

I know you are so excited about your new enrollments and that they have decided to start their journeys with a Premium Starter Kit. You have earned $25 for each of those new enrollments and life is good! Guess what? It gets better!

Young Living not only provides you with a one-time thank you through the $25 Start Living Bonus, they also provide you with another incredible bonus that can have lasting affects on your business as you grow!

The Fast Start Bonus is an enroller-based bonus that pays you, the enroller, 25% of the new enrollments' PV for the first three calendar months of their membership. Yes, 25%!

> **❝ The Fast Start Bonus is an enroller-based bonus that pays you, the enroller, 25%... ❞**

This incredible bonus is a tool that promotes providing extra support from enrollers for the first three calendar months of a new member's journey. Notice the term "calendar months." The month the new member enrolls counts as month one. For example, you enroll a new member and in that first month they purchased 100PV in product. If that 100PV was from a Premium Starter Kit you would receive $25 in bonus from the Start Living Bonus and you would also receive $25 in bonus due to the Fast Start Bonus. Isn't that an incredible bonus? Young Living not only encourages you to empower and support your enrollments, but they reward you generously for doing so!

Luckily for you, it gets better! With any network marketing business, duplication is the key to success. Young Living provides a secondary part to the Fast Start Bonus. When one of your enrollments enrolls a new member you will receive 10% of that new enrollments' PV for their first three calendar months.

The people you enroll are typically referred to as your first-level enrollments. It doesn't technically have anything to do with your levels, but it acts as a simple concept to help you understand your personal enrollments. For level 1 enrollments, when they enroll new members, I typically refer to them as my second-level enrollments.

You will earn the 10% on your second-level enrollments no matter when your first-level enrollment signs them up. For example, if you recruited Jane five years ago and Jane enrolls Julie today, you will earn 10% on Julie's PV for her first three calendar months of membership. I'm sure you can appreciate just how powerful that is!

> **" You will earn the 10% on your second-level enrollments no matter when your first-level enrollment signs them up. "**

Nitty-Gritty

If your first-level enrollment fails to place a 50PV order, then you will not be eligible to earn 10% on their enrollments.

When Fast Start is being paid on a new member, Young Living will reduce the PV of that member by 70% for all other payable commissions.

If a Retail Customer converts to a Wholesale Member, you will qualify to earn this bonus.

If a member becomes inactive at any point and reactivates, you will not be eligible for Fast Start unless their period of inactivity exceeded two years.

A maximum of $200.00 in bonus can be earned on any first-level enrollment for a given month.

A maximum of $80.00 in bonus can be earned on any second-level enrollment for a given month.

Business Tip

The Young Living compensation plan consists of two types of potential ways to earn. The first is with commissions and the second is with bonuses. I like to think of bonuses as a mechanism that promotes good business-building behavior. Take Fast Start for example. You earn by enrolling members. You continue to earn for three

> **❝ I like to think of bonuses as a mechanism that promotes good business-building behavior. ❞**

months, which promotes ensuring that your new members have all of the tools, resources, and guidance they need. You also earn as they enroll new people, which motivates you to ensure your enrollments understand how to share Young Living correctly and are equipped to duplicate your approach.

Chapter 7
EXERCISE YOUR BRAIN!

This exercise will challenge you to use all of your knowledge on Fast Start. Peek back and read the section again as you complete the exercise. Don't forget about those nitty-gritty details! Calculate the Fast Start Bonus that will be earned by the person at the top. Assume that each level 2 person in the diagram was enrolled by their sponsor.

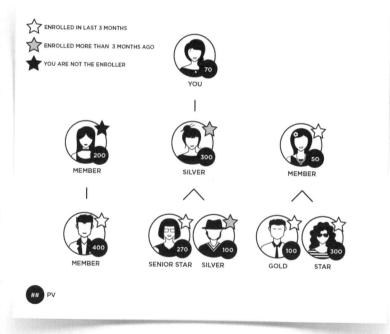

If you answered $79.50 you are doing great! If not, read the Fast Start section again and give it another try.

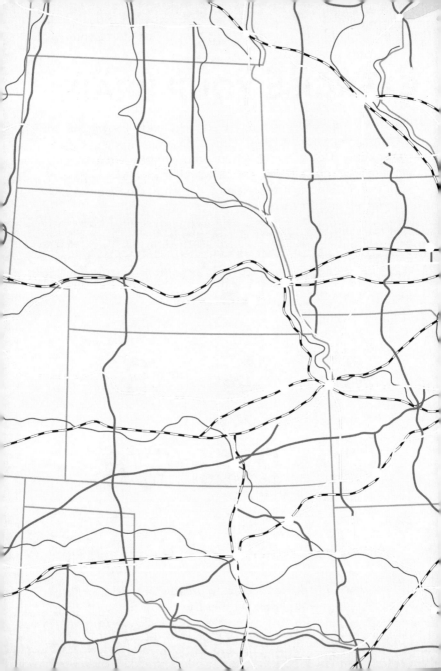

UNILEVEL COMMISSIONS

This Commission is a sponsor-based commission and you must have 100PV to qualify. When looking at your downline, you are visually looking at the sponsor lineage of your team. We refer to your personally sponsored members as your level 1. Their personally–sponsored members are your level 2. Here is a quick graphic that shows you an example of two levels.

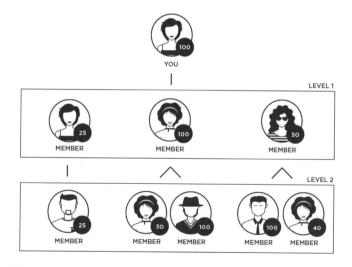

Unilevel Commissions are calculated based on the level where a member in your downline resides. The commission percentages for Unilevel are the same for all ranks in Young Living. For level 1 you earn 8%. For levels 2, 3, 4, and 5 you earn 5%, 4%, 4%, 4% respectively. The higher your rank, the deeper you earn. Starting at the rank of Distributor you earn on two levels, and as you increase in rank you earn an additional level of Unilevel until you reach Executive. No member, regardless of rank, earns more than five levels deep for Unilevel Commissions.

So, how does Young Living calculate this commission? Young Living takes a member in your downline and asks: "What level is this person to you?" If the person is your level 2, then Young Living will pay you 5% of that person's PV. If the member you are being paid on is in their Fast Start period, their PV will be reduced by 70% and you will be paid 5% of the reduced PV.

> **❝ If the member you are being paid on is in their Fast Start period, their PV will be reduced by 70%... ❞**

Remember learning about Dynamic Compression earlier? Remember how I said that the great benefit of Dynamic Compression was that it maximizes your Unilevel Commission? Let's pretend you have a level 1 member at 30PV and they have a level 1 member at 150PV. The 150PV member will virtually rollup to your level 1 since their sponsor did not place a qualifying 100PV order. This means that instead of you earning 5% on the 150PV, you will now earn 8% on the 150PV. Awesome, huh?

Chapter 8

EXERCISE YOUR BRAIN!

Leverage the knowledge you have gained on Dynamic Compression and Unilevel to calculate the Unilevel Commission earned by the person at the top of the tree.

You should have come up with $33.70 for the Unilevel Commission earned by the person at the top of the tree.

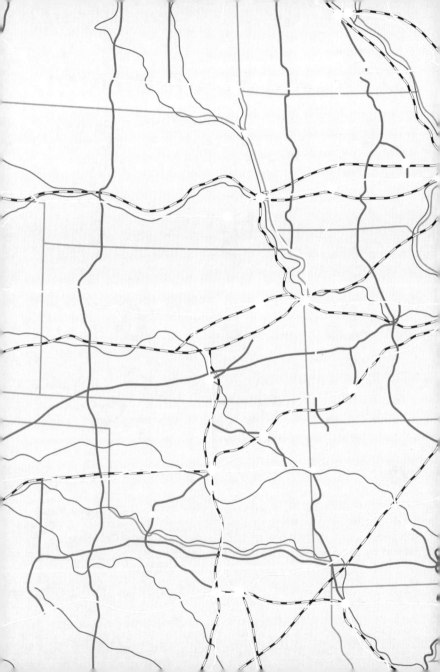

RISING STAR TEAM BONUS

Do you remember reading earlier about considering the bonuses provided by the Young Living compensation plan as a means to promote good business-building behaviors? Well, I have to admit that this bonus is by far my favorite behavior-driving bonus.

To be successful in any network marketing company, you have to love the products! Also, if you want to grow in network marketing you have to understand the power of compounding by way of duplication. As a leader, you want to identify the strategies that work well for you and are easy to duplicate for your team.

> **❝ As a leader, you want to identify the strategies that work well for you and are easy to duplicate for your team. ❞**

If you are an enrolling machine and you enrolled two new people each month, you would have a team of 25 by the end of the year. This includes you plus the 24 new team members.

However, if you focused on teaching duplication and everyone in your organization enrolled just one new person each month, you would have a much larger organization. The table on the next page shows you this concept by assuming that each month, every person in your organization enrolls just one new member.

Month	Existing	New	Total
Jan	1	1	2
Feb	2	2	4
March	4	4	8
April	8	8	16
May	16	16	32
June	32	32	64
July	64	64	128
August	128	128	256
September	256	256	512
October	512	512	1024
November	1024	1024	2048
December	2048	2048	4096

The above chart represents a perfect matrix. Practically speaking, people do not grow their business in a perfect matrix, but this is more about teaching you the power of duplication and leveraging the law of compounding. Compounding is the difference between a team of 25 or 4,096! Duplicating and teaching simple and effective strategies can have incredible impact!

Rising Star Team Bonus is the only bonus tied to you being a part of Young Living's Essential Rewards program. We have already talked about creating a discipline of participating in this program at 100PV or more each month so that you can always qualify for the maximum amount of commissions and bonuses available to you.

This bonus is a share-based bonus. If you do not understand what a share-based bonus is, don't worry! A share-based bonus means that Young Living provides you with qualifications that earn you a certain number of shares. The shares by themselves have no value. The value comes from how the actual monetary share value is calculated. For the Rising Star Bonus, Young Living takes all of the commissionable sales and uses 1% of that as the share bonus pool money for RSB. As a contrived example, assume that Young Living has $10,000,000 in commissionable sales for a given month and is going to award 2,000 RSB shares. To determine the value for each share they would perform the following:

$$(10,000,000 * .01) / 2000$$

This would make the share value for each RSB share $50.00.

With RSB you can earn up to six shares. This particular bonus is a stair-stepped bonus (three steps), meaning that you have to qualify for the first step before you can qualify for the second. You have to qualify for step two before you can qualify for step three.

Ok, let's break this thing down by the steps:

Step One
This step awards you one share if you meet the qualifications. To earn your one share you must have at least 100PV on ER and you must have three level 1 (personally-sponsored) members, each with at least 100PV on ER as well as each have at least 300 OGV.

Step Two
If you have qualified for step one and earned your first share, you can qualify for this step. In addition to the step one qualifications you need two more level 1 members with at least 100PV on ER and

500 OGV. Meeting these qualifications earns you an additional two RSB shares.

Step Three

By qualifying for step one and step two you have now earned three shares! Step three, when met, will earn you an additional three shares giving you a total of six shares. To qualify for this step you need two additional level 1 members, each with at least 100PV on ER and 1,000 OGV.

So, why do we love this bonus so much for business-building behavior? Well, I'm glad you are asking great questions! As you learned during the ranks section, only six legs are required to reach the highest rank in Young Living. If you earn all six shares of RSB, you now have seven legs on ER and all are growing OGV. Now, we have already discussed the power of duplication, and it's incredible ability to accelerate your growth. If you understand RSB and teach it to your team, they will be equipped to maximize their earnings on ER and will work hard to get their members on ER.

The data shows, generally speaking, that members will purchase two to three times as much product once they are on ER than if they aren't. Why is that? Well, as you participate in ER you are more inclined to try new products and you are more likely to introduce transfer buying as well. Encouraging

❝ The data shows, generally speaking, that members will purchase two to three times as much product once they are on ER than if they aren't. ❞

people to see the immense value in ER not only benefits them (with the points, less expensive shipping, etc.), it also benefits you as a business builder because it is sure to increase your OGV and commissions/bonuses. It is a win-win approach!

Nitty-Gritty

Compression does not affect RSB. If a level 1 member does not place a qualifying order and causes a level 2 member to compress, the compressed level 1 member can not be used as a qualifying member for RSB.

Once you receive RSB the first time, you only qualify to earn it for 24 months. This means that after 24 months you will no longer be eligible for the bonus, even if you meet the step qualifications.

This bonus is only available to Star, Senior Star, and Executive ranked members.

If you reach a rank of Silver, which causes you to lose the bonus for that given month, and in the following month you rank Executive, you can still qualify for RSB assuming you are still in the 24-month qualification period.

EXERCISE YOUR BRAIN!

Time to work your mental muscle again. In this exercise, you need to determine why the person at the top of the downline will NOT earn RSB.

Example 1

All level 1 members in this graph have 100PV on ER and also all have at least 300 OGV. The top member does not qualify because they do not have 100PV on ER.

Example 2

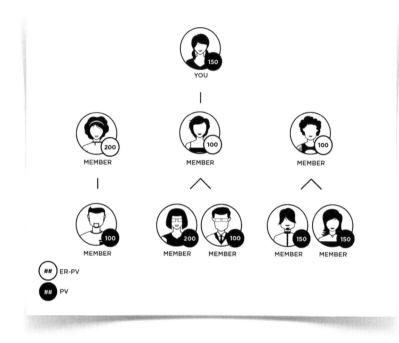

You are probably being more astute and have identified that all level 1 members have 100PV on ER with at least 300 OGV. In this example, the person at the top loves the products because they have 150PV, but as you have noticed, is not on ER!

Example 3

In this example, the person at the top does have at least 100PV on ER. However, looking at the level 1 team members, we see that one of them only has 50PV in ER.

GENERATIONS

You understand levels, right? Great! Now, forget everything you know about levels as we talk about generations. Understanding generations is key if you are to master the Young Living compensation plan for your Silver+ growth.

Your first generation, also referred to as your personal generation, is all of the members in your downline up to, but not including, the first Silver+ leader you encounter. Your personal generation is made up of members in different legs and different levels. This is why it is key to ignore levels when discussing generations.

When you view your downline in your Virtual Office, and look at a member on your level 1, first ask, "Are they a Silver+ leader?" If not, then they are part of your personal generation. When you expand their downline and look at their level 1 members, ask "Are they a Silver+ leader?" The answer for some of those members may be yes and for some it may be no. For the ones where the answer is no, they are still in your personal generation. Continue to expand their downlines until you run out of paths where you have Silver+ members. This makes

> **❝ Understanding generations is key if you are to master the Young Living compensation plan…. ❞**

up your personal generation. Each time you hit a Silver+ leader in your traversal, a new generation is created. Back to your downline. If you have a member on your level 1, and that member is a Silver+ leader, they are a part of your generation two. Continue to traverse their downline and each time you find a new Silver+ leader, they would be part of the next generation.

Here is a diagram to visualize generations.

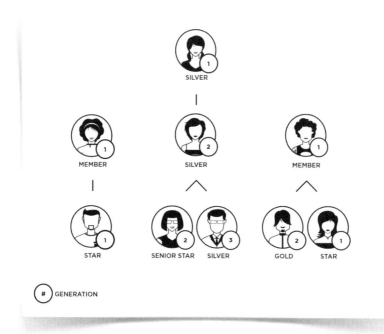

Look at the leg farthest to the left. Since there are no Silver+ leaders in that leg, they all belong to generation 1 (personal generation). As we move to leg 2, the first member is a Silver+ leader, which means they belong to generation 2. In their level 1, they have a Senior Star and a Silver. Because the Senior Star is not a Silver+ leader, they continue to belong to the generation 2 that was started by their sponsor. Their sibling Silver leader belongs to generation 3. In the leg furthest to the right, the first member is not a Silver+ member, so they continue to belong to generation 1. They have a Gold and a Star on their level 1, where the Gold belongs to generation 2 and the Star continues to belong to generation 1.

Assuming you are a Silver+ leader, a trick to determining what generation any person in your downline belongs to is to do the following:

1. Start with the number 1.

2. Find a member in your downline that you would like to determine their generation.

3. Ask the question: Are they a Silver+ leader? If the answer is yes, then add 1.

4. Find all of the members between you and the member in question, and count all of the Silver+ leaders and add that number to your total.

Chapter 10
EXERCISE YOUR BRAIN!

Using the example downline below, determine which generation each member belongs to.

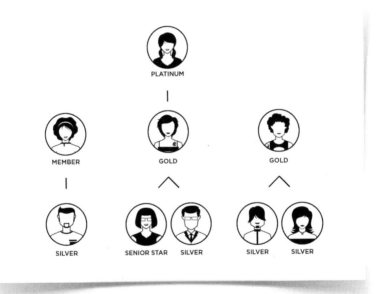

Starting with the Platinum leader at the top they belong to G1 (generation 1). The leg furthest to the left has a member which is G1 and a Silver that belongs to G2. In the middle leg, you start with a Gold leader that belongs G2. They have a Senior Star that is also G2 and a Silver that begins G3. In the leg furthest to the right we have a Gold that begins G2 who has a Silver that belongs to G3 and another Silver that belongs to G3 as well.

GENERATION LEADERSHIP BONUS

As you rank up in Young Living you will begin to notice your earnings shift from Rising Star Bonus and Fast Start to generation-based bonuses and commissions. This is intentional as generation-based compensation structures are a mechanism to promote building your business by building more leaders.

> **❝Generation-based compensation structures are a mechanism to promote building your business by building more leaders.❞**

The generation-based bonuses are available to Silver+ leaders, and even if you are not a Silver+ leader at the moment, it is helpful to know these concepts as you continue to grow your business.

The Generation Leadership Bonus is another share-based bonus where the share value is determined, like the RSB bonus, based on the commissionable sales for the month. For this particular bonus, YL uses 6.25%. For example, if Young Living awards 5,000 shares and has $10,000,000 in commissionable sales, the share value would be calculated as:

(10,000,000 * .0625) / 5000

This would create a share value of $125.00 per awarded share.

What makes this bonus stand out so much is that there is no limit on how much you can earn! So let's talk about how you actually earn these bonus shares.

As a Silver+ leader you are awarded shares for yourself as well as shares for members in your downline who are also Silver+ leaders, up to a certain generational depth. Remember when we talked about generations? That information is crucial to understanding this bonus! You begin with earning one share for yourself as a Silver leader, and as you grow in rank you earn an additional share for yourself for each rank above Silver. So for Gold you earn two, for Platinum you earn three, etc. But that is just the tip of the iceberg.

For each rank you earn on a generation depth. For Silver, that depth is three generations in total. One of those generations is your personal generation, where you earn shares on yourself. You then earn on two additional generations. Earlier, I taught you a trick to determine the generation of anyone in your downline. If you apply that trick to a member in your downline, and the resulting generation number is two or three, you also earn a share on them! As you rank to Gold you begin to earn on four generations-where the first is you and then you earn on three additional generations. As a Gold leader, when you apply the generation trick to anyone in your downline and the resulting generation value is 2, 3, or 4, you will earn shares on that member! You can see that as you reach Royal Crown Diamond, where you earn on a total of eight generations, your Generation Leadership Bonus can become a huge part of your monthly earnings.

> **❝ Your Generation Leadership Bonus can become a huge part of your monthly earnings. ❞**

Nitty-Gritty

When earning Generation Leadership Bonus, you can only earn as many shares on someone in your downline as you can earn for yourself. Meaning, if you are a Gold leader with a Platinum leader in a generation you get paid on, you can only earn two shares on that Platinum leader because you can only earn two shares for yourself as a Gold leader.

EXERCISE YOUR BRAIN!

Calculate the number of Generation Leadership Bonus shares earned by the member at the top.

Example 1

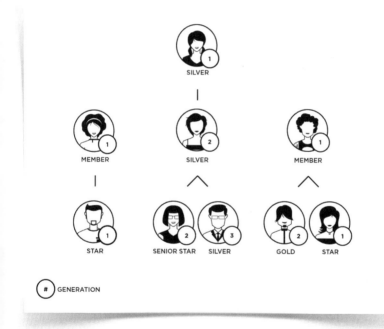

You should have calculated four total shares. You will first earn one share for yourself. Your next two shares come from the two Silver leaders in the middle leg. Lastly, you earn one share on the Gold member in the leg furthest to the right. This is because you can not earn more shares on a member than you earn for yourself.

Example 2

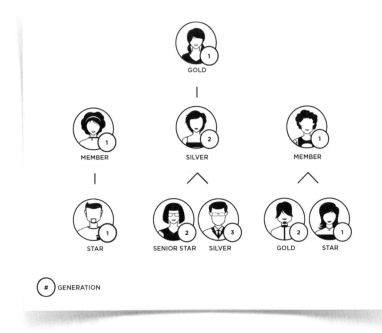

GOLD

MEMBER   SILVER   MEMBER

STAR   SENIOR STAR   SILVER   GOLD   STAR

(#) GENERATION

You should have calculated six total shares. As a Gold leader you will earn two shares for yourself. Your next two shares come from the two Silver leaders in the middle leg. Finally, you earn two additional shares on the Gold leader in the leg to the far right.

GENERATION LEADERSHIP COMMISSION

This commission structure is similar to the Generation Leadership Bonus because it leverages the same understanding of generations. For each Silver+ ranked member, you can earn up to a certain generational depth. For Silver, you earn on three total generations, and for each rank beyond Silver the depth increases by one, up to a total of eight generations at Royal Crown Diamond level.

This commission structure pays a percentage of the volume for each generation, and the percentages for each generation are the same. The difference is that as you rank up, you earn deeper. The generation commission percentages are: 2.5%, 3%, 3%, 3%, 3%, 3%, 3%, 1%.

A very important point to make about Generation Leadership Commission is that the percentage paid is NOT on the OGV (cumulative PV) of the generation. This commission structure is affected by Fast Start and if the member in a particular generation is in their Fast Start period, their PV is reduced by 70%. Let's walk through an example. Let's say you have three people in generation one, which you earn 2.5% on. Two of the members have 100PV and enrolled over a year ago. The third member also has 100PV and enrolled last month. You would get paid as follows:

$$(100 + 100 + (100 * .30)) * .025$$

Your Generation Leadership Commission on this generation would be $5.75. This of course is a contrived example, as you would have many more people in your generation one and at

Silver would also earn on two additional generations.

If you wanted to calculate this commission by hand, you would use the generation trick you learned earlier and find out the generation of every member in your downline. Then, you would take every member with a generation value of one and add up all of the PV (taking Fast Start into account) and multiply the resulting PV by 2.5%. You would follow the same process for those with a generation value of two, and you would multiply the resulting cumulative PV (taking Fast Start into account) by 3%. You would continue this process until you have calculated the commissions for all of the generations you qualify to earn on. In the end, you would add up the results for each generation.

Chapter 12
EXERCISE YOUR BRAIN!

Generation Leadership Commission can be a tricky commission to calculate. Let's do two examples. In the first we will assume that everyone in the downline is not in their Fast Start period. In the second example, you will need to leverage all your your wits to calculate the commission.

Example 1

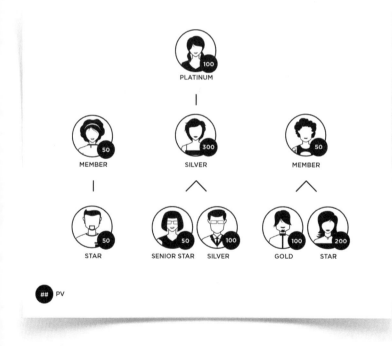

Answer: You should have calculated a Generation Leadership Commission of $27.75 (11.25 + 13.50 + 3).

Example 2

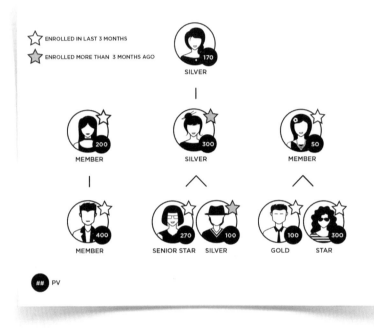

Don't let your mind explode! Take this one piece–by–piece. You first want to find all of your generation one members and begin to add up their PVs, making sure to adjust the PV for Fast Start. Do this for each generation, and when you are done with that step, you can multiply the cumulative PV's by the appropriate percentage. Total all of the PV's and you should get an answer of $26.71.

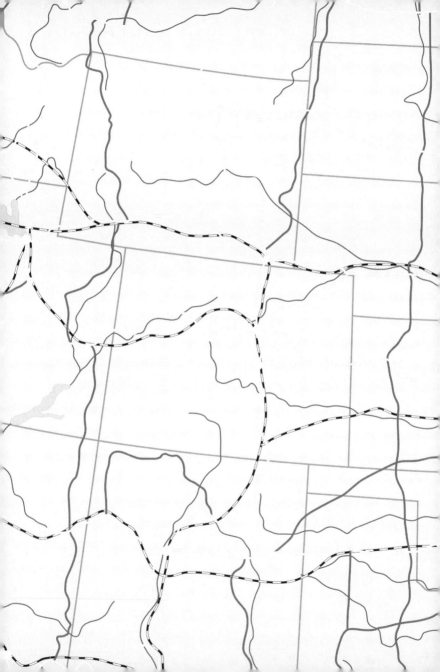

Chapter 13

PROFESSIONAL ACCOUNTS

Young Living has a third membership type that we have not discussed. Professional Accounts are members who wish to purchase Young Living products for the purpose of resale. Professional Accounts purchase products at a deep discount and because of this, the commission structure is slightly different. Professional accounts pay commissions in the same manner as Unilevel, except that the PV for Professional Accounts is reduced by 50% before calculating.

It is worth noting that when looking at your virtual office, the PV reduction has already taken place.

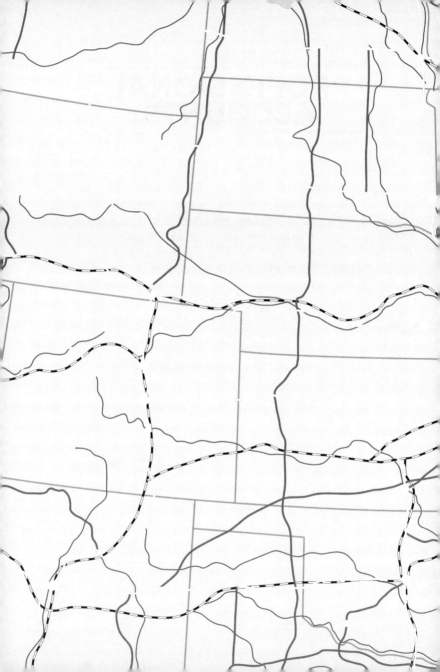

Chapter 14

DIAMOND LEADERSHIP BONUS

The Diamond Leadership Bonus is also a share-based bonus available to Diamond+ leaders in Young Living. The share value of the bonus is calculated in the same manner as the RSB and Generation Leadership Bonus is calculated. The percentage of commissionable sales allotted for this bonus is 0.5%.

As a Diamond leader you earn one share of Diamond Leadership Bonus, and for each advancing rank, you earn an additional share. You can earn a total of three shares as a Royal Crown Diamond.

There are additional qualifications required to earn this share, such as attending the International Grand Convention or attending a Winter/Spring Harvest and the Diamond Retreat.

Chapter 15

OILYTOOLS

I hope that by reading this book you have gained a deeper appreciation for the financial opportunity provided to you by Young Living. There are numerous ways to earn income and the potential for abundance is truly limitless.

As I am sure you are now aware, calculating your earnings can be challenging, and as your team grows the task is practically impossible to do correctly. This is where OilyTools really shines!

OilyTools is an application that will take the burden of calculating your estimated earnings away and also provides you with numerous other features to help you grow and manage your Young Living business.

The most-loved feature of OilyTools is that it calculates your estimated earnings for the current month multiple times a day for all ten Young Living ranks. Everything you read in this book, along with many other nuances of the compensation plan, are used to determine your current estimated earnings in almost real time. You can even change ranks to see what you could be earning at higher ranks, or take a moment and look at what you were making at previous ranks.

To learn more about OilyTools and start your subscription, visit http://www.oilytools.com.

Carrier 🤝	2:27 PM	▬
	OilyTools	⟳

○ ●
July
Last Updated: Jul 21 1:15 pm

	9999 NEW MEMBERS	**999,999** ORG. GROUP VOLUME
	Rank: Platinum	⟩

NAME	PERCENT	AMOUNT
● Customer	99.00%	$999.99
● Starter Kit Bonus	99.00%	$999.99
● Rising Star	99.00%	$999.99
● Fast Start	99.00%	$999.99
● Unilevel	99.00%	$999.99